WHO IS
THE WIDOW'S MUSE ?

Also by Ruth Stone

IN AN IRIDESCENT TIME 1959
TOPOGRAPHY AND OTHER POEMS 1971
CHEAP - NEW POEMS AND BALLADS 1975
SECOND-HAND COAT - POEMS NEW AND SELECTED 1987, 1991

WHO IS
THE WIDOW'S MUSE ?

Ruth Stone

◯ Yellow Moon Press ◯
Cambridge, Massachusetts

ISBN: 0-938756-32-X

Copyright © 1991 by Ruth Stone

Some of the poems in this work
have previously appeared in
Poetry East and *Boulevard.*

Illustrations & front cover by Phoebe Stone
Back cover photo by Jan Freeman
Production & design by Robert Smyth

Yellow Moon Press
P.O. Box 1316
Cambridge, MA 02238
(617) 776 - 2230

For Kandice Lombard
who asked the question

All Time Is Past Time

Goliath is struck by the stone.
The stone turns into a bird.
The bird sings in her window.
Time is absurd. It flows backward.
It is married to the word.

This is the window of the giant's eyes.
This is the bird singing alone.
This is the river of forgetting.
This is the chosen stone.
This is Goliath's widow.

Struck by the stone he leaps
into the future. He lies
a monolith, a rune, light
from a distant nova. Not even a bone
remembers begetting him ever.

The song is a monotone.
She is the word and the window.

I

Crow, are you the widow's muse?
You wear the weeds.
Her answer, a caw.
Her black beads:
two jet eyes.
A stick fire
and a thorn for her body.
Into the wind, her black shawl.

II

Sedated, tranquilized,
the widow is cut loose.
She rises in a basket
attached to a multicolored balloon.
It hauls her up,
her little casket,
into black blue frenzied gas molecules.
Below, her miniature house,
her small heavy car,
fixed on a square of grass,
disappear.

III

Even the trash-can looks possible.
On certain days the muse can change
into brown plastic.
The womb of sorrow.
All your spoiled leftovers
scraped into this mouth.
The widow's muse has an omnivorous appetite.

IV

The widow thinks to herself,
"The muse of bones.
The innocence of cartilage."
And she walks down the street,
stripping the flesh from faces.
"We love their sockets," she says.

V

Is he the muse?
The fire irons
remind the widow of his grave.
Down or up?
The devil smiles benevolently.
"We all love him," he says,
ashes falling from his teeth.

VI

What is this impatience
the widow says every morning—
Who's here?
Nevertheless,
she brews the coffee,
looks through the cupboards.
Today she won't try to be clever.
Everything has a flat patina
like a dirty window.
The widow's muse is probably
a char woman with a hangover.

VII

The widow talks to him frequently,
saying, "If you had been here
this wouldn't have happened."
After which she goes to the refrigerator.
Ice cream has a calming effect.
The muse may prove to be simply fat.

VIII

"Am I, then, the widow's muse?"
cries the widow.
"Is alone more alone
than I was led to believe?"
The sexton takes her hand.
He is willing to dig the hole,
he says—
to do the dirty work,
but that's it.
If she want to have a second coming,
she's going to have to raise it
on her own.

IX

The widow gathers her children
into the kitchen.
Here are the pots and pans,
she tells them.
Here are the lentils
and carrots and onions.
Here is the old place for sorrow.
The children are here now,
she thinks;
but what about tonight?
The muse rises in steam
and disappears.

X

Hidden toward the back,
the widow tries
to feel part of a larger thing.
If asked,
she is quick to agree.
Never mind
if you can shoot a bean
through one of her ears
and have it come out the other.
She pretends she is a manikin
in a department store window.
See and be seen,
is her motto.
Perhaps the widow's muse
is her dead mother.

XI

The stone fountain is fluted
like a shell without Venus.
Its thin hair-crystal
spews, melting and weeping.
Here the widow's muse
thinks of being a frog.
All she really wants to do
is croak.

XII

All night the widow dreams
of the muse.
In the morning the field is white
with dew-beaded spider webs.
"I am both a monster
and a soft vulnerable body,"
she says.
"Is the muse the inexorable
law of death?
Is my claim to the muse
no more than my own breath?"

XIII

Alone in the car,
the widow makes songs to him.
She tells him her secrets.
The body of the car holds her;
it is not silent,
it too sings and responds.
She wonders if the muse is the car.
She and the car have
sculptured a comfortable place.
Her feet are at home.
Her hands clasp the steering wheel.
Her eyes seek the way
and the car knows.
Then why has she named the car
Violet Hunt?
The widow sighs. Here it is again—
gender and sorrow.

XIV

Even her stockings, even her shoes,
wept for him.
Her shoes in their pockets
noticed he no longer
knocked them aside.
He is dead, they dreamed,
what is the use of the bows on our toes?
The widow thought,
"Were hints of the muse hidden here?
Could the muse be fetish?
Could it be footwear?"

XV

The widow wraps her arms around
her own shoulders.
She shivers.
"I am no more than a sack,
an internal worm,
a bloody computer," she says.
"But somehow, the soles of my feet
are sad. 'Where have we been?
Where are we going?'
they call up to me."
The widow refers them to the muse.
"Oh, oh," the widow thinks,
"here we go again. Shoes!"

XVI

The widow has, unfortunately,
grown curious and is reading
The Egyptian Book of the Dead.
(Modern edition.)
It makes her nervous to think
of all those women
drinking poison
and lying down in the chamber
outside the sealed room
where the Pharaoh's body,
a resinous shell, packed
with oils and perfumes,
and wrapped in oil-soaked cloths,
is all prepared for their journey.
But then,
she was nervous when
she bought that double plot.
"Oh, if only
he hadn't done this,"
she says.

XVII

The widow keeps erratic hours.
If she goes to bed at nine,
she is wide awake at three.
She gets out of the snarled bed
and feels her way to the toilet.
Her kidneys function.
Could the muse reside in the bladder?
The widow put this
ridiculous notion aside.

XVIII

I must be serious, the widow thinks,
I must face reality.
This isn't a temporary separation.
(Perhaps the widow's muse is expectation.)
Actually the widow thinks he may be
in another country in disguise—
that one day he will come back.
He was only fooling.
That was someone else that they buried.

XIX

Is the widow's muse
all the women of the world?
The widow runs her hands
over their faces,
like braille.
She reads them with her palms.
How complex they are.
They are as rich as sea broth.
Their minerals sparkle in the air.
"We sift through time
like the diatoms," she says,
"we multiply and add to ourselves.
Ai-yi, ai-yi!"

XX

The Widow's Song

As I was a springbok,
I am a leper.
As my skirt lifted up as a veil,
so the shawl of a widow.
As the oxlip,
so the buffalo grass.
As the wall of a garden in winter,
so was I, hidden.
As the game of the keeper . . .
not counted.
So I am without number.
As the yellow star grass.

XXI

The widow likes to wash sheets
and hang them on the line.
They are definite areas,
flexible squares,
tangible comfort.
The wind plays with them.
The widow likes to wrestle with
the body of sheets.
As she subdues them to
folded compact units,
and stores them in the linen closet,
she feels the muse may
dwell in the linen closet.

XXII

"Perhaps we are born widows,"
the widow thinks.
"Perhaps that is our basic condition.
Those lemmings are always
throwing themselves into the sea.
They run around looking
for a way out.
Widows don't enjoy being strong.
Widows want to be delicate as a scarf
laid in a scented cedar box.
Yes," she thinks,
"the muse is a key."

XXIII

The widow looks at her shelves
of the world's great poetry.
She studies anthropology.
She takes courses with young men
who are writing their dissertations.
"There is a way out of this forest,"
she says,
"even though the birds have eaten
my trail of bread crumbs."

XXIV

Every Saturday the widow shops.
She goes to Ames, Kings,
Bargain World.
She knows, in a way, that
she is looking for substitutes.
But she no longer buys sheets
and sleeping garments.
"If it's plastic, it's plastic,"
she quips;
and she tries on moon boots.
She feels that the muse
likes to shop.
The widow's muse
may be—a shopping cart.

XXV

Repetitious, repetitious,
every day is like another.
Waste not,
want not.
The widow becomes a vegetarian.
After a few months she notices
that carrots scream.
"Listen," she says,
"patience, patience.
Can I live on mineral water?
Can the muse be an amoeba?"

XXVI

In the guest room the widow
looks at her feet.
She is wearing borrowed
fake fur bear claws.
Outside the last snow is
rising along the light.
"Everything will disappear,"
she thinks.
There is no past.
Even the widow's muse
is subject to these laws.

XXVII

The widow lies on the bed
and looks out the window.
It is snowing in Buffalo.
She can't complain.
She is warm, well fed,
though she has never been to Spain.
She grew up mainly on the plain—
in Indianapolis . . . not that it mattered.
So much for Greek mythology—
Rex Harrison and Leslie Howard.
But the muse,
was she once a marble statue?
Was she painfully shattered?

XXVIII

The widow's friends
put her on the train.
At the moment of parting
she realized:
they are me;
I am them!
"Oh, the poor things,"
she said,
meaning all three . . .
the beautiful woman,
the brilliant man,
and herself.
The muse let a single tear
slip from its closed eyes.
"We are not amused,"
it muttered.

XXIX

The widow likes to ride on trains.
Trains are phallic symbols.
The engineer is probably on crack.
His speed outruns the antiquated equipment.
These trains were built for middle-aged engineers.
Once she and her husband
were fooling around on a train.
They were trying to torment
four old men playing cards.
The men's eyes were heavy lidded.
They looked at their hands.
Could the widow's muse be carnal?
Could she have hot pants?

XXX

Going past Utica
the widow is reminded
of the cotton mills.
Almost a century of Utica sheets
and pillow cases;
the great brick buildings
blackened with soot.
The widow's knowledge of all this
was gleaned largely
from old stereoscopic cards . . .
double pictures of girls
standing in long rows
with their long hair hanging down
their backs and their long skirts
and their white waist shirts,
tending the long rows of looms.
Some of them were
sending their brothers to college.
"Yes, it's true," the muse sighs.

XXXI

It came to the widow
that she was a courier;
just as the cirrus clouds
puffed like sudsing underwear,
the snow cut off short of Rensselaer,
and the cab drove over the pedicled
cement arches into Albany.
It was this time of year he died.
She has been showing him the sky
over and over since then.
"The widow's muse is a city pigeon,"
the rising widow murmured.

XXXII

The widow is having Mott's apple juice
on the bus.
It reminds her of God's first garden.
Just as they pass through Troy,
she catches a glimpse of
Eve and Helen.
They are probably seventeen.
Tomorrow is the first day of spring.
Everyone on the bus is a senior citizen.
The widow's muse decides to
have hysterics.
Could the widow's muse be envious?

XXXIII

The widow felt immortal.
She couldn't help it.
The blue so unpredictable;
the cliffs, dynamited to
make room for the road, so
ruggedly square.
The houses so pretentious
and shabby.
"It's my entire life bare of memory!
It's the effect of March!"
The muse lay thin as light.
"I'm worn out," she said.
"Don't abuse me."

XXXIV

The sun is coming through the ice patterns
on the window.
The widow is home.
She takes a picture of her dog
on the worn out Persian carpet.
All night the widow dreamed of houses
and who owned them.
A deep sense of enclosure
comes over the widow.
"I will never be ignorant again,"
she says.
The muse lifts her eyebrow.
"Illuminations, final statements,
nutshells," the muse cries . . .
"blather, blather, blather!"

XXXV

The widow thought—
What do these gestures mean:
the quick feel of your own hair-do,
the top of your head?
Is it vanity?
Is it to keep your brains
from leaking out?
The widow's muse snickered,
"It may be submission . . .
it may be a code of presenting . . .
it may be an effort to
keep him from dragging you
off to his cave!
Don't you wish!" she said.

XXXVI

Now it is summer.
Under the blackberry bushes,
an empty beer can.
It is rusted,
but it smells of him.
The widow puts it
in a plastic bag
and hides it in the attic.
Could the muse be effervescent?

XXXVII

The widow thinks about the photograph
of toothless Maude Gonne
standing outside a polling booth.
How shameless she is,
tall and thin,
that political skeleton;
that lover of military men.
And the widow knows
that for a temporary time
Maude Gonne was the muse
of William Butler Yeats,
that Maude Gonne was Ireland.
And the widow McBride . . .
who was her muse?
Who was the muse
of all that flesh
gone to waste?

XXXVIII

It's time for coffee.
The long night is done.
She creaks out of bed;
puts her feet on the bristly carpet.
I need oil on my joints,
the widow thinks.
I didn't relax last night.
The widow used to be able
to sleep eleven hours
when she wasn't a widow.
Sleep was delicious then,
even languid.
Even their quarrels
were dreamlike.
"The widow's muse
certainly lives in Eden,"
the widow said.

XXXIX

The muse is mad.
It keeps digging him up
to check his identity.
It measures his leg bones,
his hips.
All the tools of passion
have melted like wicked broth.
There is only the clean calcium.
Even the marrow
is calcified sponge.
The widow decides there is
nothing about him
that isn't sweet.

XL

"Ho, ho, ho,"
the widow's muse said.
"Ha, ha, ha.
I'm giving you a hint."
"Never mind," the widow answered.
"I may go on a cruise.
I may bicycle through Nepal.
I may change my sexual preference."

XLI

Bees are calculated widows,
spiders are near-sighted widows;
was I involved
in my darling's demise?
The result of this inner
flagellation
was a headache.
The widow went to bed.
"It's enough to drive one
to self abuse!
Give me a valium,"
the widow's muse said.

XLII

After thirty years
the widow gets smug.
"Well, I did it,"
she brags,
"with my own bare hands."
The muse shrugs.
"Uh-huh . . .
Did what?"
The muse leads her to
a back stairway.
There is his undershirt
in an old trunk.
"Smell that," the muse says.
The widow inhales his lost perspiration.
"You brute," she whimpers.
The muse takes a bone
out of her arm
and knocks the widow senseless.
"She'll never learn,"
the muse simpers.

XLIII

The widow wonders if she
is here on false pretenses.
Is this really her home?
After all, if he saw her now,
would he marry her?
The widow pinches the fat
on her abdomen.
There is dust on all the furniture.
Her fingernails are not clean.
The muse has deserted her.
"If you are not good enough
for him," the muse says,
"why should you be
good enough for me?"

XLIV

The widow looks at spring catalogues.
She feels a need to dig in the garden;
to eat, in the summer, the large
male flowers of the squash,
the ones that will not bear fruit.
She longs for stuffed squash blossoms.
This symbolic cannibalism
is a negative resurrection,
a logical illogic.
She allows herself in a dream
to lie along the ground
under a canopy of three-foot-
long green beans.
The muse is on vacation.
The widow gets a card from the muse.
"Am playing tennis everyday with
Don Hall, Don Justice, Don Juan."

XLV

The widow puts on her Long Beach
Literary Women's Festival shirt.
Stained with coffee, it keeps
her company in bed.
That's where we wear our scars
and badges, anyway, she says.
The widow's muse was at the Festival, too.
She was that one with iron grey hair
and the large manilla envelope of poems,
who sat next to the widow at dinner.
"Don't read those scary poems," the widow
said. "There are five hundred women here,
and they know all that.
Just get up and give them the old soft shoe."

XLVI

The widow thinks, "Is this
all there is?"
No one hears her.
No one sees her.
She realizes that life
exists in minute details,
packets of energy,
the signal moment of awakening.
"Those dreams," the widow cries,
"they are never clear.
And all the rest just goes by.
Is the muse the test, the proof
that I was here?"
The widow's muse holds the notebook
behind her back.
Sometimes the widow's muse
is shy.

XLVII

The widow wonders—
does a story exist like a chair?
Is a bed a story without words?
Am I an anachronism?
The muse held the widow's hands.
"There, there," the muse said
in a low trembling voice,
"you've been watching those
late T.V. movies
in lonely motels."
"I too want to levitate,"
cried the widow, distraught,
yet strangely calm.
The muse unplugged the widow
from her life support system.
"Better you should be dead,"
the muse said.

XLVIII

The widow knew it was morning.
A grey light filtered through
a crack in the heavy drapes.
I am too fat for a swimming suit
in a motor lodge, the widow thought.
She saw her body like a trained
porpoise, leap through the green
water of the kidney shaped pool.
"No doubt, a rich public life
awaits me," the widow cries.
"I must not hide in room two-fourteen.
That's what this is all about."
Is the widow's muse the dangerous
highway and empty corridors?
"The natives were restless last night,"
the muse complains . . . checking out.

XLIX

When the snow melts the widow discovers
her yard is a dump.
Where have all these strange
things come from?
The slimy insides of an oil filter
lie on the spears of daffodils.
An exhaust pipe like a rusty snake
is hidden in the forsythia.
The widow's house is close to the road.
She is reminded of the farmer next door
who rolls his rocks onto her land.
"Vermont is a Greek Island," the widow says.
The widow's muse wraps her head in a veil.
"Basta, basta," the muse cries,
"you begin to understand!"

L

The widow accumulates meaningful trash.
She is no different than all the others.
"I should set aside a room for a shrine.
And how am I going to throw away their little toys?"
She joins the long line of sentimental mothers
waiting for phone calls.
Increasingly, the widow enjoys her grandchildren.
Sometimes she pauses to tell her dead husband . . .
"It's that time of life when we
should be taking a cruise; going to Europe;
going to Australia. But it's just as well.
The grandchildren need me.
You would have liked them, too."
The muse yawns. The muse is irritable.
"Yes, yes," the muse says;
"So what else is new?"

LI

It is Easter.
The widow wakes up to rain
on the roof. The basement is flooded.
The furnace is out.
"The only thing that is risen here
is the water," she says to herself.
"Once I was an egg.
A soft vulnerable X.
Possibly capable of parthenogenesis.
Then I was penetrated
by a renegade Y.
Then I developed into this . . .
a widow. But before then,
I wasn't a widow.
Before then I was a sun
lighting up the dark descent
into the Fallopian tube.
I was autonomous.
I had come from forever."
"What a lot of drivel you are
talking," says the muse.
"Just quit it . . . which
came first, the chicken or the egg?"
The widow looked thoughtful.
"Actually," the widow says,
"I think it was the rabbit."

LII

The widow is told by a great seer
that fifty-two is a magic number.
She consults the muse.
"We must get into a higher gear,"
the muse whispers. "We must shift
out of this phase."
"Just one more about shoes,"
the widow begs.
The muse shakes her head.
"No. We must get back to the real thing.
The blood and meat of the world."
The muse took the widow in her arms.
"Now say it with me," the muse said.
"Once and for all . . . he is forever dead."